Book 2

learn to play the oboe!

A carefully graded method
that emphasizes good tone production,
builds a sound rhythmic sense and
develops well-rounded musicianship.

by James MacBeth

Play all warm-ups very slowly.
Observe all dynamic markings.
Listen to yourself.
Take frequent rests.

WARM-UP

NOTE: In keeping with the system of abbreviations used in
Learn To Play The Oboe, Book 1, the following will
be used as reminders in Book 2:

        R   = finger with little finger of right hand

        L   = finger with little finger of left hand

        ½H   = use half hole position

        F Key = use regular fingering for F

        Fork = use fork fingering for F

        TOK = use thumb octave key

        SOK = use side octave key

THE RAKES OF MALLOW

Irish Folk Tune

*DUET

KUTTNER

*In all classic transcriptions in duet form throughout this book, the bottom line is generally of less technical difficulty than the top. Either or both parts may be assigned by the teacher according to the proficiency of the student.

Teacher-Student duets can provide excellent EXPERIENCES FOR LEARNING.

WARM-UP

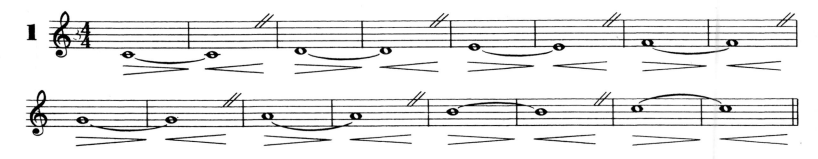

FINGER FLEXER

Practice both slow and fast.   Use a firm finger action.   Repeat many times.

SMOOTH CONNECTIONS IN C

HALF-HOLE REVIEW

Practice No. 4 using both left and right E♭ fingerings.

Left side E♭   Right side E♭

   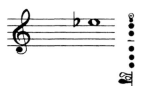

TSCHAIKOWSKY MELODY

Lento (quite slow)

SARABANDE

Con moto (With motion)

BOISMORTIER

$\frac{3}{8}$ indicates 3 counts in each measure, ♪ = 1 count.

WARM-UP

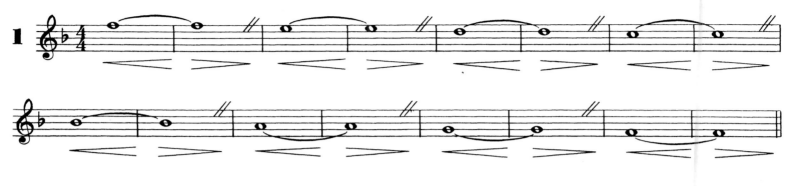

ETUDE IN G

HALF-HOLE HASSLE

VERY HIGH NOTE REVIEW

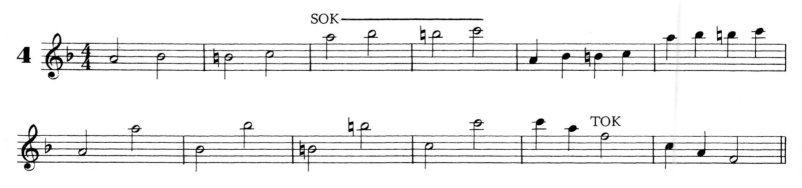

PRAYER FROM "HANSEL AND GRETEL"

HUMPERDINCK

* *poco a poco* = little by little.   *poco a poco cresc.* = gradually louder and louder.

SIXTEENTH NOTE DUET

J. M.

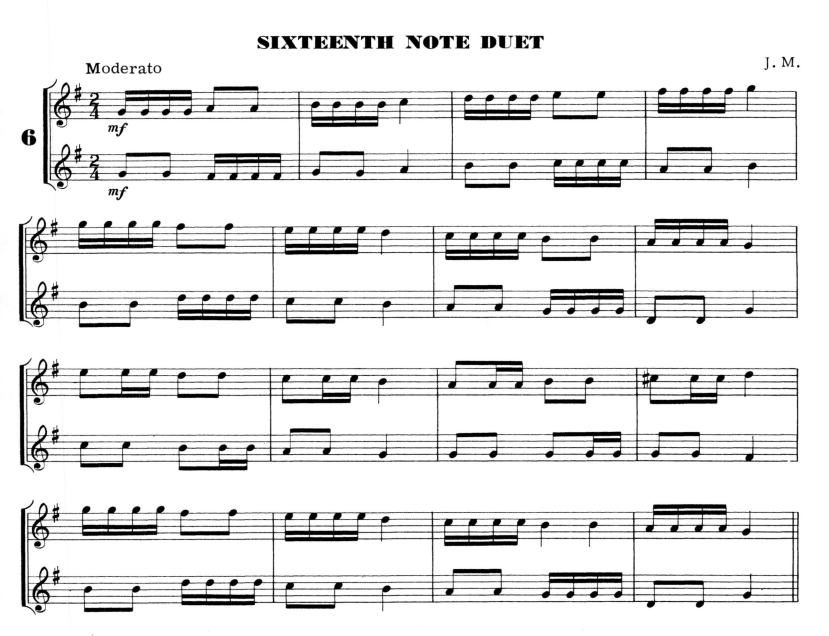

WARM-UP

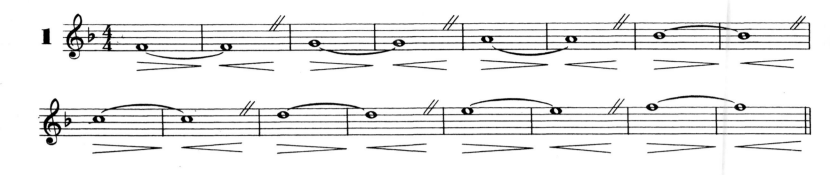

FINGER TWISTER

Practice both slow and fast.   Use firm finger action.   Repeat many times.

MELODIOUS ETUDE

RHYTHMIC ROUNDUP

GIGUE

BOISMORTIER

WARM-UP

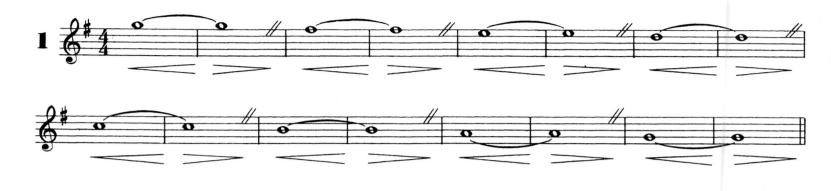

THE BUSY B

ROUND

SMOOTH CONNECTIONS IN G

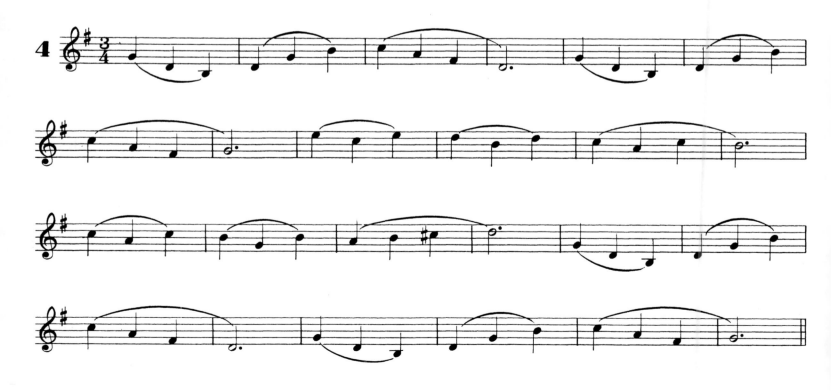

TURKISH MARCH

BEETHOVEN

RHYTHMIC DUO

J. M.

WARM-UP

1

ETUDE IN D

Allegro moderato

2

FIVE SCALES AND CHORDS YOU SHOULD KNOW

3

C Scale

C Chord

G Scale

G Chord

D Scale

D Chord

F Scale

F Chord

Bb Scale

Bb Chord

LITTLE SERENADE

BRAHMS

CAREFUL COUNTING DUET

J. M.

WARM-UP

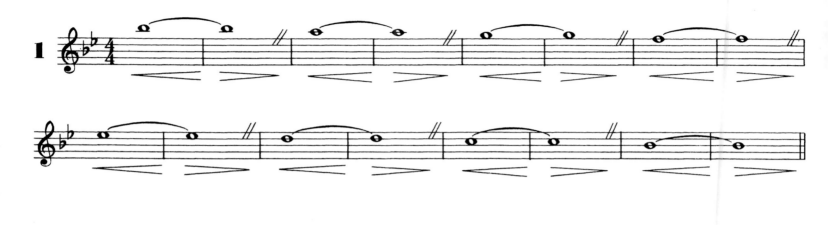

THE BUSY B (Flat)

ROUND

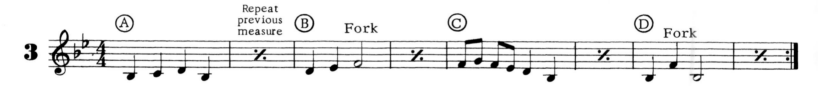

SMOOTH CONNECTIONS IN Bb

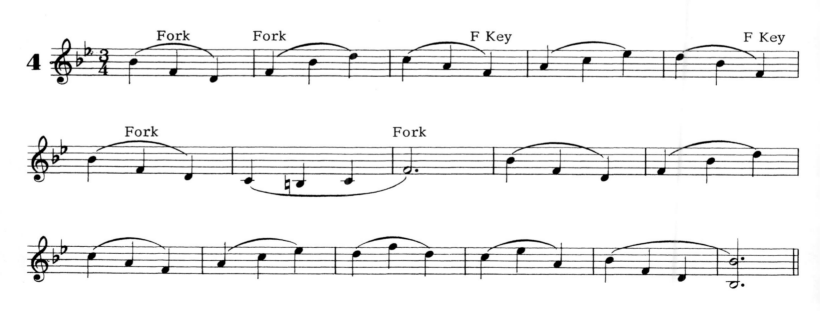

* Student model oboes sometimes have no low Bb key.
If your instrument does not have this key, omit exercises 2 and 3.

MINUET

BACH

WARM-UP

THE KEY OF Eb

EXERCISE IN Eb

THREE BLIND MICE

*In keys of two or more flats the Fork F Fingering should always be
used between Eb and F. Much if not most band music is in flat keys.

MINUET

Moderato

MOZART

sempre legato (always in a connected style)

CUT-TIME CAPER

Allegretto

J. M.

17

WARM-UP

TECHNIQUE DRILL

Practice slowly with firm finger action.

SMOOTH CONNECTIONS IN Eb

LITTLE SONG

Andante

MOZART

MUSETTE

BACH

WARM-UP

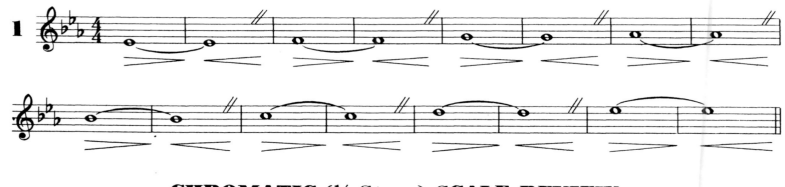

CHROMATIC (½ Steps) SCALE REVIEW

Practice both tongued and slurred.

ENHARMONIC STUDY

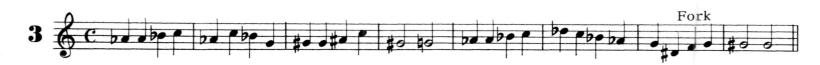

CHROMATIC ETUDE

*Left side E♭ should be used here to avoid sliding
little finger.   See bottom of page 4 for review.

GAVOTTE

SIXTEENTH NOTE REVIEW

WARM-UP

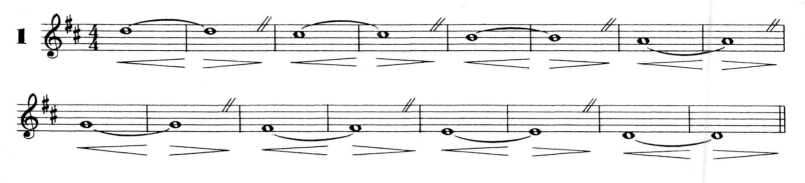

CHROMATIC FINGER EXERCISE

Practice slowly with firm finger action.

WALTZ

J. M.

Waltz tempo *(One beat in a measure)*

F Key   Fork

From beginin to the end
We'll be there for each other
Know wonder why we're all known as brothers
We be smokin what
We be smokin what they call that purple haze
This is what we always blaze

Welcome to fredonia
doin somethin mean fo it
come wit me, cuz I like dudes

MARCH

STUDY IN SYNCOPATION

J. M.

23

WARM-UP

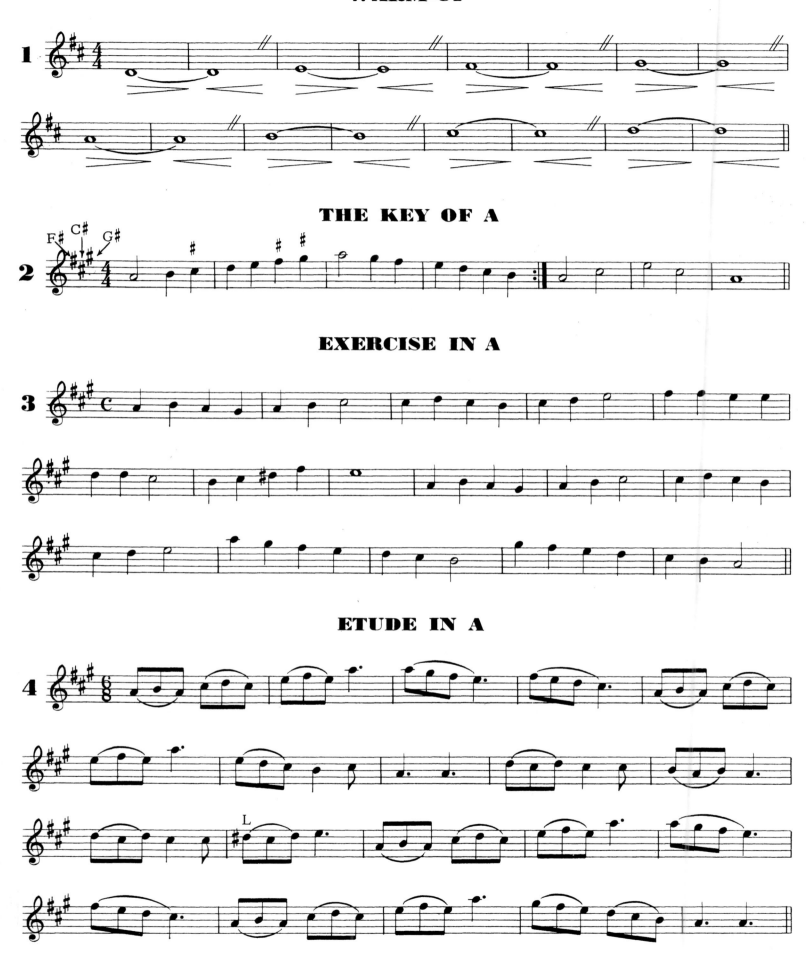

THE KEY OF A

EXERCISE IN A

ETUDE IN A

MENUET

BACH

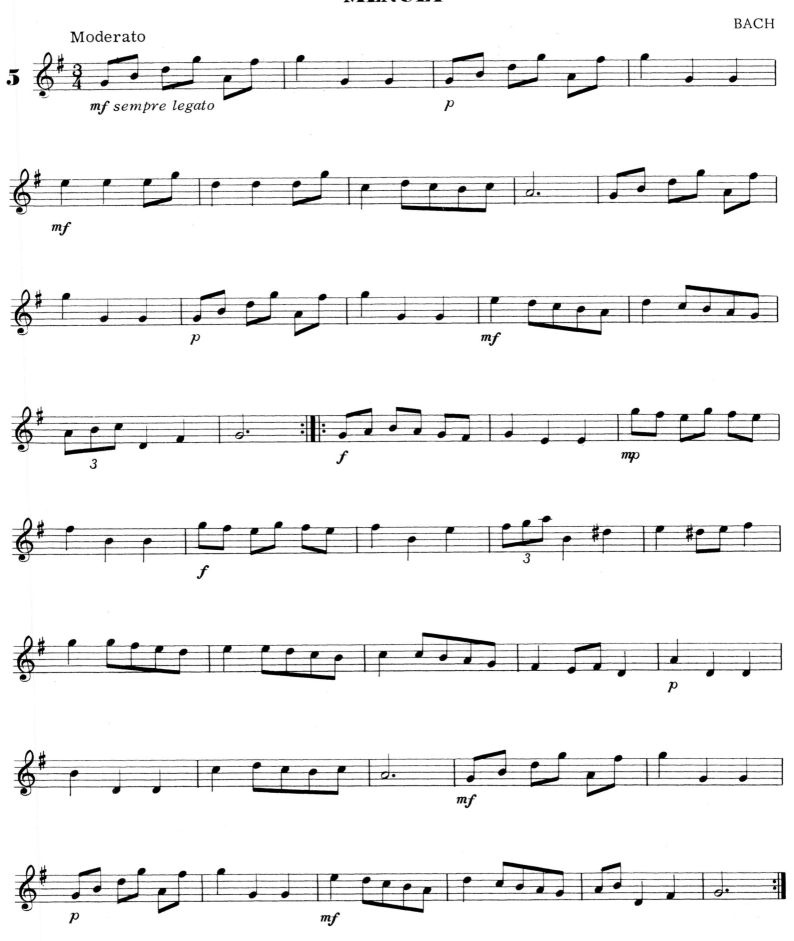

WARM-UP

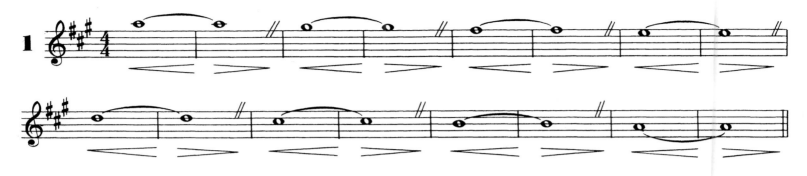

FINGERING EXERCISE

Practice slowly with firm finger action.

SMOOTH CONNECTIONS IN A

CHROMATIC SCALE REVIEW

Practice in both C and ¢

18th CENTURY HUNTING SONG

Con spirito *(With spirit)*

5

WARM-UP

KEY OF E

LITTLE SONG IN E

ROUND

SONATINA

BEETHOVEN

RHYTHMIC REVIEW

J. M.

* The most commonly used grace note is the *Acciaccatura* or short grace note. It is played as quickly as possible and usually takes its time value from the note before. The accent is given to the note to which it is attached. A single short grace note has a fine diagonal line crossing its stem.

WARM-UP

ETUDE IN E (Major)

Compare this with No. 3.

ETUDE IN E (Minor)

What form of the Minor is this?

A MINOR SCALE has a different sequence of half and whole steps than does the major scale. There are three forms of MINOR SCALE: the NATURAL FORM, the HARMONIC FORM and the MELODIC FORM. Study and play the following examples. Listen to them carefully. Discuss with your teacher the differences between MAJOR and MINOR.

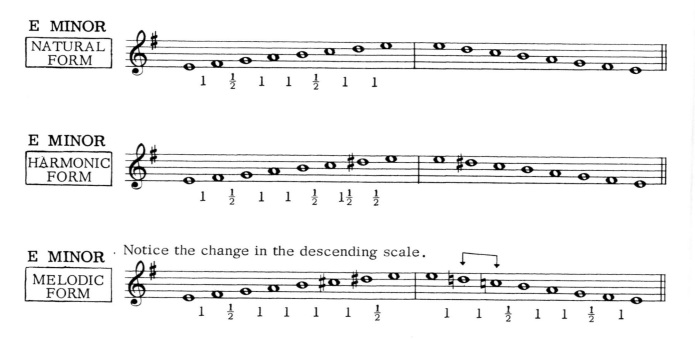

GAVOTTE IN D MINOR

HAAG

WARM-UP

KEY OF B

SHORT TUNE IN B

SWEET BETSY FROM PIKE

Andantino (*In 1)

American Folk Song

*When any of the triple meters: $\frac{3}{4}$, $\frac{3}{8}$, or $\frac{3}{2}$ are played at a fast tempo, it may be inconvenient to count each beat.   When speed is essential, each measure should receive one beat.

BAGATELLE

BEETHOVEN

WARM-UP

1

ETUDE IN B

2

SAME TUNE — MANY KEYS

Key of _____   Key of _____

3

Key of _____   Key of _____

Key of _____   Key of _____

Key of _____   Key of _____

*Can you name each
of these Major keys?*

33

BOURRÉE

HANDEL

CANON FOR THREE

A Canon is a composition in which one voice imitates another.
The combination of these parts creates harmony.

SCHUBERT

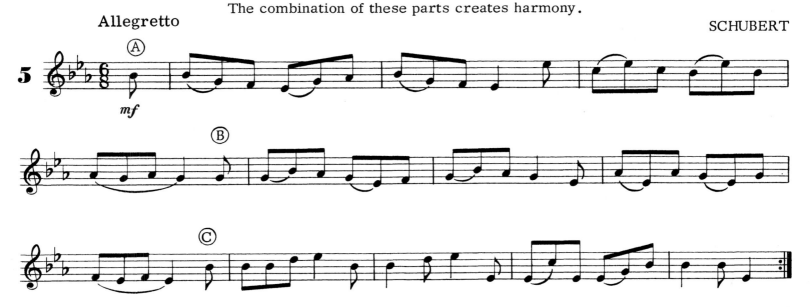

WARM-UP

KEY OF Ab

SMOOTH CONNECTIONS IN Ab

LULLABY

BRAHMS

TAMBOURIN

AUBERT

Giocoso (*In a playful style*)

5

Fork

WARM-UP

FINGERING EXERCISE IN Ab

Practice slowly with firm finger action.

MENUET

BACH

*long
grace note

*Written   Played

Frequently used in music of the old masters, the *Appoggiatura* (often referred to as long grace note or classical grace note) is rarely found in modern music editions. This ornamental note usually takes one beat of the value of the note which it precedes. The accent falls on the Appoggiatura rather than on the note to which it is attached. Notice that it does not have a fine diagonal line crossing its stem.

ROMANZA

BEETHOVEN

Leggiero *(Lightly)*

Double grace notes are played either ahead of the beat or on the
beat depending on the style, character or tempo of the music.

WARM-UP

KEY OF Db

WALTZ IN Db

*TRILL STUDY

*The *Trill* (sometimes called a shake) marked *tr* or *tr*〰〰 is executed by a rapid alternation of the printed note with the next note of the scale above it.

DUET IN BAROQUE STYLE

WARM-UP

FINGERING EXERCISE

Practice slowly with firm finger action.

SONG IN THE KEY OF Db

WEBER

Semplice (*In a simple style*)

mp *sempre legato*

SONG IN THE KEY OF D

Compare this with No. 3

MENUETT

LEOPOLD MOZART

5 Con vivo (*In a lively style*)

THE MINOR AND THE MAJOR

J. M.

6 Vivace

WARM-UP

TWO NEW SCALES (Which sound the same)

The order of flats and sharps in the key signature is always the same.

Flats in this order ──────→ B E A D G C F ←────── Sharps in this order

Two New High Notes

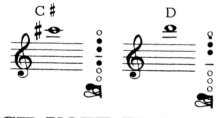

HIGH NOTE EXERCISE

BARCAROLLE

Dolce *(Sweetly)*

OFFENBACH

Practice in each octave.

DUET

KALLIWODA (adapted)

SCALE AND CHORD REVIEW

FINGERING CHART

● — Means to close hole or press down key.

○ — Means hole or key is left open.

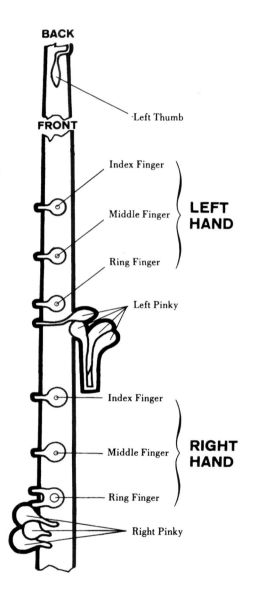

BACK

Left Thumb

FRONT

Index Finger
Middle Finger
Ring Finger

LEFT HAND

Left Pinky

Index Finger
Middle Finger

RIGHT HAND

Ring Finger

Right Pinky

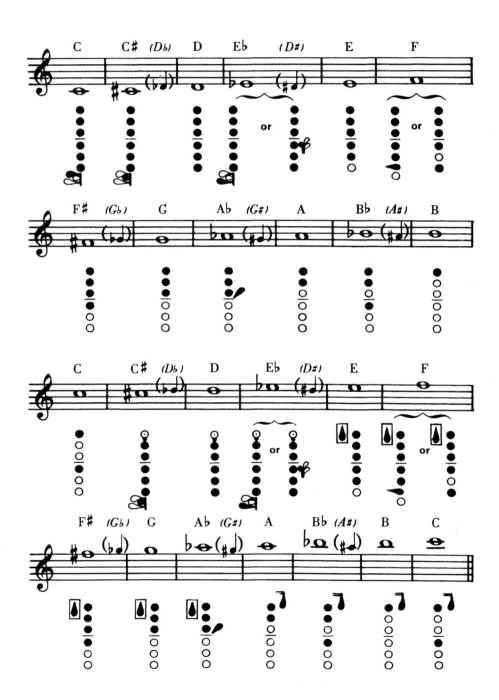

A Small Dictionary of Musical Terms

SPEED

Accelerando (accel.). . . . . Speeding up
Adagio . . . . Slow and deliberate
Allegretto . . . . A bit slower than allegro
Allegro. . . . . Lively and fast
Andante . . . . "Walking speed" . . . . . comfortable
Andantino . . . . A little faster than andante
Grave . . . . Slow, serious
Larghetto . . . . A little faster than Largo
Largo . . . . Slow, broad and solemn
Moderato . . . . A moderate speed
Prestissimo. . . . . As fast as you can play
Presto. . . . . Very fast
Vivace . . . . Brisk . . . fast
Remember that all tempo markings are *relative*

DYNAMICS

cresc. or ———————— . . . . *crescendo* . . . . getting gradually stronger (louder)
decresc. or ————————— or **dim.** . *decrescendo* or *diminuendo* . . . . getting gradually weaker (softer)
sf or sfz . . . . *sforzando* . . . . . with sudden emphasis
ff. . . . . *fortissimo* . . . . . very strong
f. . . . . *forte* . . . . . strong
mf . . . . *mezzo-forte* . . . . moderately strong
mp . . . . *mezzo-piano* . . . . moderately soft
p. . . . . *piano* . . . . . softly
pp. . . . . *pianissimo* . . . . . very quietly

STYLE

Accel.. . . . . *accelerando* . . . to speed up gradually
A tempo. . . . . in the original speed
Dolce . . . . sweetly
Legato . . . . smoothly, connected
Leggiero. . . . . lightly
Maestoso . . . . majestically
Poco. little
Poco a poco . . . . little by little
Rit. . . . . *ritard* . . . to slow down gradually
Simile . . . . the same as before
Sostenuto . . . . sustained
Staccato. . . . . separated
Tenuto. . . . . held out to full value